D1422909

1

Knowsley Library Service

Please return this book on or before the date shown below

Knowsl@y Council

- 4 FEB 2017

1 ~ MAR 2017

2 1 APR 2017

1 6 DEC 2017

You may return this book to any Knowsley library
For renewal please telephone:

Halewood 443 2086; Housebound Service 443 4223;
Huyton/Mobile 443 3734/5; Kirkby 443 4290/89;
Page Moss 489 9814; Prescot 426 6449;
School Library Service 443 4202;
Stockbridge Village 480 3925; Whiston: 426 4757

http://www.knowsley.gov.uk/

Have fun with Arts and Crafts

Rita Storey

W
FRANKLIN WATTS
LONDON•SYDNEY

First published in 2012 by
Franklin Watts
338 Euston Road
London NW1 3BH

Franklin Watts Australia
Level 17/207 Kent Street
Sydney NSW 2000

Copyright © Franklin Watts 2012
All rights reserved.
Series editor: Amy Stephenson

Packaged for Franklin Watts by Storeybooks
rita@storeybooks.co.uk
Designer: Rita Storey
Editor: Nicola Barber
Crafts: Rita Storey
Photography: Tudor Photography, Banbury
www.tudorphotography.co.uk

A CIP catalogue record for this book is available
from the British Library.

Printed in China

Dewey classification: 745.5

ISBN 978 1 4451 1070 7

Cover images Tudor Photography, Banbury

Franklin Watts is a division of Hachette Children's Books,
an Hachette UK company
www.hachette.co.uk

Before you start

Some of the projects in this book require scissors, paint, glue
and a sewing needle. When using these things we would
recommend that children are supervised by
a responsible adult.

KNOWSLEY LIBRARY SERVICE	
270969401	
Bertrams	01648884
J745.5	
SV 12.2.13	

Contents

Big Cat Masks

Tigers and lions are big cats that live in the wild. They move very fast and have a fierce roar. Disguise yourself as a tiger or a lion with these colourful paper masks and see how loudly you can roar!

For tiger and lion masks you will need

Both masks

- A4 sheet of thin white card
- scissors
- glue
- black felt-tip pen
- hole punch
- elastic

Tiger

- A4 sheets of thin orange, yellow and black card

Lion

- A4 sheets of thin yellow, dark brown and pale brown card
- dark brown felt-tip pen

1 Use the mask shape on pages 30 – 31 to draw a tiger mask on to the thin white card. Cut out the shape. Ask an adult to help you cut out the eye holes. Trim the shape so that it is just wider than your face and so that you can see through the eye holes.

2 Place the mask template on to a piece of thin orange card and draw round the shape. Remember to cut out the eye holes as well.

3 Use the template on page 30 to cut a snout shape from thin yellow card and a nose shape from thin black card. Glue the snout on to the front of the mask under the eyes. Glue the nose shape at the top of the snout.

4 Use the templates on pages 30 – 31 to copy the shapes of the stripes and the inside of the ears on to thin black card. Cut them out. Glue them on to the tiger's cheeks and ears as shown.

Lion

   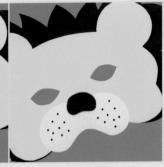

1 Follow steps 1 – 2 of the tiger instructions, using the lion mask shape on pages 30 – 31 and the thin yellow card.

2 Use the template on pages 30 – 31 to cut out a mane shape from thin, dark brown card. Spread a thin line of glue on to the inside edge. Glue the mane on to the back of the mask.

3 To make the snout and nose, follow step 3 of the tiger instructions, but this time use the pale brown card for the snout shape and the dark brown card for the nose shape.

4 Use a dark brown felt-tip pen to draw dots on the snout.

Tiger and Lion

1 To finish off your tiger and lion masks, punch a hole on either side of each mask.

2 Thread a piece of elastic through the two holes and tie it to fit your head.

3 Slip the knot to the back of the mask. Put on the mask to disguise yourself as a fierce tiger or lion.

Rrrrrrrrrrrrrrooooooaaaaaaarrrrrrrrrrrr!

Bendy Monkeys

This troupe of cute little monkeys would love to come and play with you. Their arms, legs and tails are made of bendy pipe cleaners so they can hang out almost anywhere.

For a bendy monkey you will need

- 3 pipe cleaners
- fabric glue
- large pom-pom
- small pom-pom
- paper and felt-tip pen
- scissors
- googly eyes

1 Twist two of the pipe cleaners together two-thirds of the way down. The long bits are your monkey's arms and the short bits are the legs.

2 Bend back 2cm at the end of each pipe cleaner. Then twist each end back round the pipe cleaner to make a loop (as shown).

3 Bend half way along the legs and arms to make the knees and elbows of the monkey.

4 Bend back 4cm of the third pipe cleaner and twist to make a loop. Position the loop between the arms and on top of where the other two pipe cleaners meet, as shown. Wrap the long end round the twisted pipe cleaners a couple of times. Leave a long piece at the back. This is the tail of the monkey.

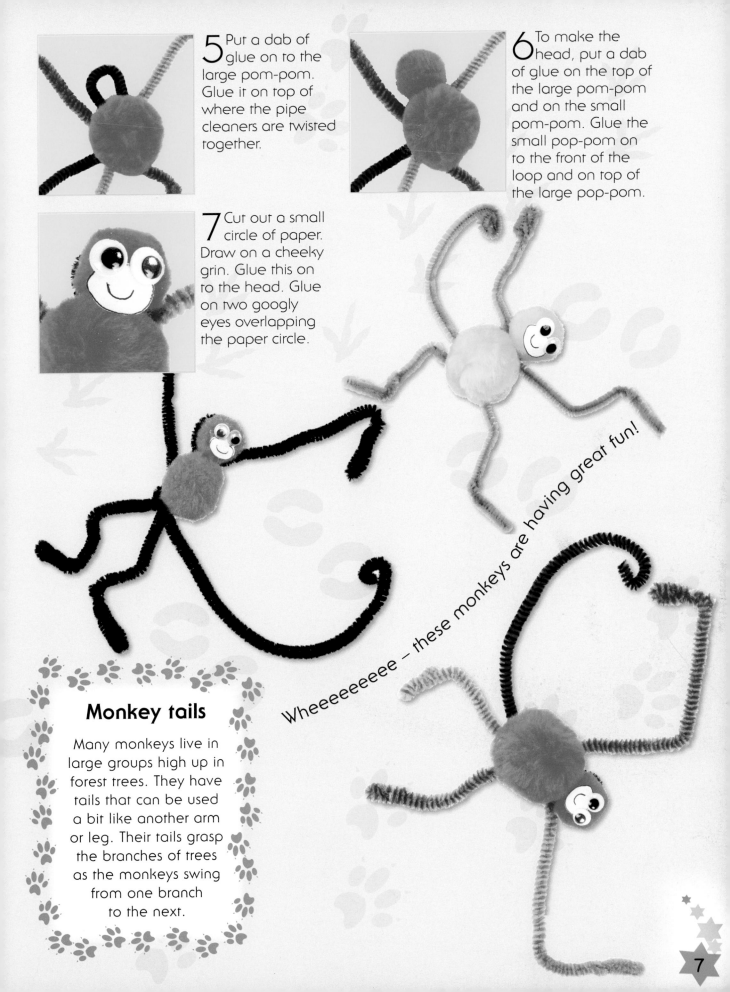

5 Put a dab of glue on to the large pom-pom. Glue it on top of where the pipe cleaners are twisted together.

6 To make the head, put a dab of glue on the top of the large pom-pom and on the small pom-pom. Glue the small pop-pom on to the front of the loop and on top of the large pop-pom.

7 Cut out a small circle of paper. Draw on a cheeky grin. Glue this on to the head. Glue on two googly eyes overlapping the paper circle.

Wheeeeeeeee – these monkeys are having great fun!

Monkey tails

Many monkeys live in large groups high up in forest trees. They have tails that can be used a bit like another arm or leg. Their tails grasp the branches of trees as the monkeys swing from one branch to the next.

Japanese Fish Kites

In Japan, families hang up fish-shaped kites outside their houses on Children's Day – 5 May. The kites flutter in the breeze and look like real fish swimming in a stream. You can make these pretty fish kites to hang up in your own window.

For a Japanese fish kite you will need

- 2 sheets of yellow A4 paper
- pencil
- compass and ruler
- card
- coloured paper
- colourful magazine pages
- scissors
- glue
- crêpe paper cut into 6 long strips 2cm wide
- ribbon to hang up the fish
- stapler
- plastic cup 8cm in diameter

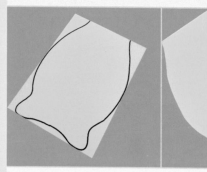

1 Using the template on pages 31 draw a fish shape on the first piece of yellow paper. The top of the shape (the mouth of the finished fish) should be along the short, straight edge of the paper. Cut it out.

2 Use this shape as a template to cut out an identical shape from the second piece of yellow paper.

3 Lay out the two fish shapes so that they are so that they are side-by-side.

Koi carp

Koi carp are colourful fish, similar to goldfish in shape but with whiskers on either side of their mouths. Carp are strong swimmers and can swim upstream against powerful currents. Because of this, carp are a symbol of determination, strength and courage in Japan. Japanese people often keep carp in ornamental ponds in their gardens.

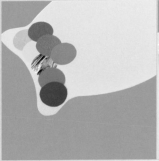

4 Using the compass and pencil draw a 4cm circle on to the card. Cut it out.

5 Using the card circle as a template, draw round it 80 times on to the coloured paper and magazine pages. Cut out all of the circles.

6 Starting at the tail end, glue 39 circles on to each of the paper shapes, overlapping them to look like fish scales. Keep the remaining two circles to one side. Leave to dry.

7 Turn one shape over and spread a 1cm strip of glue around the edge, except for the straight top edge (the mouth of the fish). Stick the ends of the crêpe paper strips on the glue at the bottom of the fish. Then place the second shape on top of the first so that the fish scales are on the outside. Leave to dry.

8 Staple the ends of the ribbon to either side of the mouth of your fish. Glue the two remaining spots near the open end to make the eyes.

9 Slide the plastic cup into the hole at the top to make the mouth open.

10 Use the ribbons to hang up your fish.

Watch your colourful fish dancing in the breeze.

Horse Puppet

This cute horse puppet can walk, trot and nod its head. You could make up a tale about a horse, then use your puppet to act out your story in a show. You could make two puppets: one for you and one for a friend.

For a horse puppet you will need

- cardboard tube from a kitchen roll cut in half, with one piece cut in half again
- scissors
- masking tape
- white and black paint
- paintbrush
- compass
- 2 pieces of thin string 15cm long
- 12 x 1cm strips of kitchen paper
- glue
- 2 pieces of black cord 24cm long
- yellow wool
- lolly stick
- 2 googly eyes

1 Take one of the short pieces of cardboard tube and cut it along the length of the tube. Then roll the tube back together so that one end is narrower than the other. Tape in place with masking tape.

2 Paint the long tube and the rolled tube white. Leave to dry. Paint black markings on both tubes.

3 Paint a black strip on to the narrow end of the short tube to make a nose. This will be your horse's head. Leave to dry.

4 Ask an adult to make a small hole in the centre of each tube with the compass point. Tie a knot in one of the pieces of thin string and thread it through the hole so that the knot is inside the tube. Repeat for the second piece of string.

5 To make hooves, paint a strip of kitchen paper with glue. Wrap the strip round the end of one of the pieces of black cord. Glue two more strips and wrap them round the first one, making the shape wider at the bottom. Repeat with the other three ends of the cord. Leave to dry. Paint the four hooves black. Leave to dry.

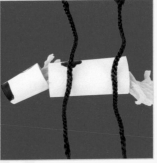

6 Join the wider end of the small tube to the body with a piece of masking tape. (The join should be on the opposite side to the holes you made in step 4.)

7 Glue some lengths of yellow wool inside the top of the long tube for the tail.

8 To make the mane, glue some lengths of yellow wool inside the top of the short tube, directly above the masking tape that joins the body to the head.

9 Dab glue on to the middle of both pieces of black cord. Glue them to the bottom of the body tube (on the opposite side to the hole) as shown.

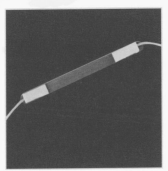

10 Tape the ends of the string to either end of the lolly stick.

Clip clop, clip clop!

11 Wind the string round the lolly stick so that the horse is standing level. Glue a googly eye on either side of the head.

12 To make your horse move, hold the lolly stick and gently move it from side to side or up and down.

Cartoon Animals

Create a whole menagerie of cartoon animals using just a few simple shapes and a little bit of imagination. When you have drawn these animals, think about how you would create even more!

To draw these animals you will need

- paper
- black felt-tip pen or a pencil
- crayons in lots of different colours

Dog

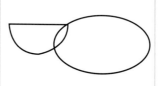

1 Draw an oval for the body. Draw half an oval for the head.

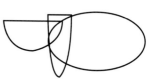

2 Add a long half oval for the ear.

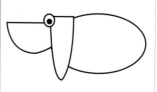

3 Draw a circle for the eye. Draw a dot inside the circle for the pupil of the eye.

4 Draw two rectangles for the legs. Draw a rounded rectangle for the tail. Colour in the dog.

Cat

1 Draw an oval on its side for the head. Draw an oval for the body. Do not draw the part that overlaps the head.

2 Draw two small circles for eyes. Put a dot inside each one. Draw two circles side by side for the nose.

3 Draw a smaller oval inside the big one. Draw two ovals for feet.

4 Draw two triangles for ears. Draw in a nose, tongue and tail. Colour in the cat.

Cow

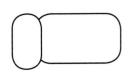 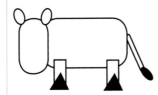  

1 Draw a rounded rectangle for the body. Draw another rounded rectangle for the head.

2 Draw two rectangles for legs. Draw triangles for the hooves. Draw a thin rectangle with a thin oval at the end for the tail. Draw two more ovals for the ears.

3 Draw a half circle and two rounded rectangles for the udder. Draw an oval for the nose. Add two small ovals for the nostrils inside the large oval.

4 Draw two circles for eyes and put a dot inside each. Colour in your cow.

Pig

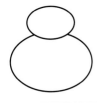  

1 Draw a small oval for the head. Draw a large oval for the body. Do not draw the part that overlaps the head.

2 Draw a small oval inside the head for the snout. Draw two dots on the small oval for nostrils.

3 Draw two dots for eyes. Add two triangles for feet. Draw two triangles for ears.

4 Colour in the pig. Add a curly tail.

Penguin

1 Draw an oval for the body. Draw a circle for the head.

2 Draw a smaller oval inside the body. Draw a small oval for the beak. Draw two ovals for feet.

3 Draw a dot for an eye. Draw an oval on each side of the body for the wings.

4 Colour in the penguin.

Flippy Frogs

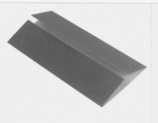

Fold these flippy frogs from colourful origami paper and decorate them with stick-on spots. Give them a flip and watch them leap on to the lily pad.

1 Fold the paper in half. Unfold. Fold both sides into the middle.

2 Fold the top corners into the middle. Crease the folds. Unfold the corners.

To make a flippy frog you will need

- square of green origami paper 21cm x 21cm
- stick-on spots
- piece of green paper
- scissors
- pen or pencil

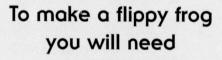

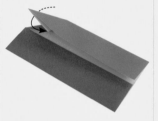

3 Push the top corners in on themselves on both sides to form a point at the top.

4 Fold both sides into the middle.

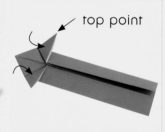

top point

outer point

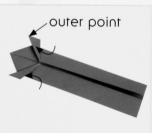

5 Fold the top points down and out to make an arrow shape. Crease the fold.

6 Fold the outer points upwards so that the flap is folded in half with the point facing upwards.

Small frogs jump better but are more difficult to fold. Once you can fold this jumping frog easily, try to make one with a smaller square of paper.

7 At the other end of the shape fold the corners in. Crease the folds. Unfold the corners.

8 Push the bottom corners in on themselves on both sides to form a point at the bottom.

9 Hold the top of the points. Pull the points up and out so that the paper lies flat.

10 Crease the fold as shown above.

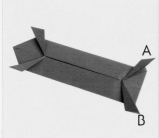

A

B

11 Fold the outer points (A and B) downwards so that the flap is folded in half with the point facing downwards.

12 Turn the shape over. Fold the bottom up level with the points of the flaps. Crease the fold.

13 Turn the shape over. Fold the bottom up again the same amount as in step 12. Then turn it over and fold it up again.

14 Cut a lily pad shape out of green paper as shown.

15 Decorate the frog with stick-on spots. To make the frog hop, press the base of the folds quickly. Play a game to see how quickly you can make your frog jump on to the lily pad.

To play the game with a friend make a second frog in a different colour.

Croak...croak....croak!

Egg Box Bugs

Ahairy spider and a wiggly caterpillar – both of these creepy crawlies are easy to make from an egg box.

To make these egg box bugs you will need

Spider

- cardboard egg box
- scissors
- black paint and paintbrush
- 4 black pipe cleaners
- scrap of white paper
- glue
- 2 googly eyes

Caterpillar

- cardboard egg box
- scissors
- yellow and green paint and paintbrushes
- 4 small pom-poms
- glue
- pipe cleaner
- 1 large pom-pom
- 2 googly eyes

Spider

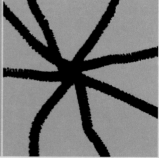

1 Cut one section out of the egg box. Trim it to leave only the part that holds the egg. Paint the outside black. Leave to dry.

2 Twist the four pipe cleaners together in the middle to make eight legs.

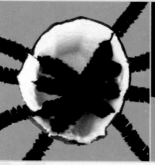

3 Turn the egg box section over and cut eight slits, four on each side. The slits should be about 5mm deep. Put the twisted middle part of the pipe cleaners in the centre of the egg box section, then press a pipe cleaner into each slit.

4 Cut some pointy teeth out of the scrap of white paper. Turn your spider the right way up and glue the teeth on to the bottom of the face. Glue on two googly eyes above the teeth.

Caterpillar

1 Cut four sections out of the egg box. Trim it to leave only the part that holds the egg.

2 Paint two sections yellow. Paint the other two sections green. Leave them to dry.

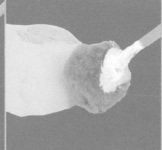

3 Dab a blob of glue on to a small pom-pom. Press the glued part on to the side of a yellow egg box section. Dab a blob of glue on to the opposite side of the pom-pom.

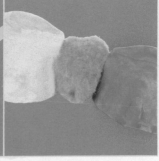

4 Press a green egg box section on to the glue so that the pom-pom is sandwiched between a yellow and a green section. Keep joining the egg box sections and small pom-poms. The last small pom-pom should be at the end.

5 Fold the pipe cleaner in half. Roll the ends back on themselves to make antennae.

6 Dab a blob of glue on to the back of the folded pipe cleaner in the middle. Press it on to the front egg box section.

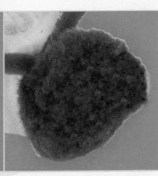

7 Dab a blob of glue on to the large pom-pom and press it on to the front egg box section, covering the bottom of the pipe cleaner.

8 Glue the googly eyes onto the large pop-pom to finish the caterpillar's head.

Furry Hamster

This cute hamster is soft and furry, just like the real thing. It has beady eyes, long twitchy whiskers and little pink toes. The hamster is easy to sew and makes an ideal pet!

For a furry hamster you will need

- A4 sheet of thin white paper
- felt-tip pen
- orange fur fabric
- cream fleece fabric
- scissors
- needle and orange thread
- teaspoon
- uncooked rice
- 1 black bead
- 2 blue beads
- white thread
- small square of pink felt

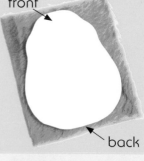

front

back

1 Trace the hamster body template on page 31 on to a sheet of white paper. Cut it out.

2 Draw round the template on to the fabric. Cut out one piece of orange fur fabric and one piece of cream fleece fabric.

3 Put the fleece and fur shapes on top of each other with the furry sides together. Stitch around the outside 5mm from the edge using back stitch and the orange thread. (see page 32).

4 Leave a 2cm gap unstitched. Turn the shape inside out so the furry sides are now on the outside.

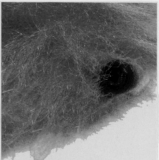

5 Use the teaspoon to fill the shape two thirds full with rice. Close the hole with two or three stitches so that no rice can fall out.

6 To make the nose, glue a black bead on to the orange fabric at the front of the shape.

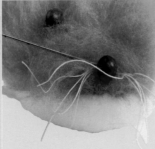

7 To make the eyes, glue a blue bead on either side of the shape just above the nose.

8 To make the whiskers, use a needle to thread short lengths of white thread through the shape just behind the nose so that the same amount sticks out on each side.

9 Trace the hamster feet template and the hamster ear template on page 31 on to a sheet of white paper. Cut them out.

10 Use the templates to cut out four feet from the pink felt and two ears from the cream fleece fabric.

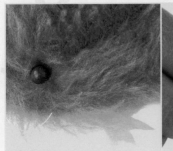

You can use small buttons for the eyes and nose instead of beads. Try using other types of fabric to make lots of different hamsters.

11 Put a blob of glue on to the short edge of each pink foot. Glue a foot on to the underside of the hamster – one in each corner. The toes should be sticking out as shown.

12 Put a blob of glue on to the straight edge of one of the ear shapes. Pinch it together and hold it for a minute or two until it sticks.

13 Repeat with the other ear. Glue the ears on to either side of the head, above the eyes, with the unfolded side facing the middle of the body.

Squeak…squeak…squeak

Pom-pom Animals

With a body puff or some net and a few scraps of card and felt, you can make these fun farm animal friends.

For a pom-pom animal you will need

Sheep

- A4 sheet of stiff black card
- ruler
- 2 x A4 sheets of thin black card
- scissors
- sticky tape
- glue
- body puff
- sheet of white paper
- pen or pencil
- 2 googly eyes

Chicken

- 1 metre strip of net 5cm wide
- elastic band
- thin yellow card
- red felt
- sheet of white paper
- pen or pencil
- 2 googly eyes

Sheep

1 Cut a rectangle of stiff black card 7cm x 4cm. Cut four strips of thin black card 4cm x 5cm.

2 To make the legs, roll a thin strip of card into a tube and tape together with sticky tape. Repeat with the other three pieces of card.

3 Put a dab of glue around one end of each tube.

4 Glue the tubes on to each corner of the rectangle of black card. Leave to dry.

5 Turn the rectangle over so that the legs are underneath. Spread the top of the rectangle with glue. Put the body puff on to the glued surface. Leave to dry.

6 Trace the sheep face template on page 30 on to a sheet of white paper. Cut it out. Use the template to draw a sheep face on the thin black card. Cut it out and glue it on to the front of the body puff, directly above one of the pairs of legs. Glue on two googly eyes.

Chicken

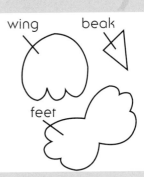

wing   beak

feet

1 Fold over 2cm of the strip of net. Turn the strip over and fold 2cm back the other way. Keep doing this until all the strip is folded.

2 Twist an elastic band tightly round the middle of the folded net.

3 Fluff out the folds to make a pom-pom.

4 Trace the wings, feet, and beak templates on page 30 on to a sheet of white paper. Cut them out. Use the template to draw a pair of feet, two wings and a beak on the yellow card. Cut them out.

comb

5 Put a blob of glue in the middle of the feet and press the pom-pom on to them. Put a blob of glue on to the triangle and press it on to the middle of the pom-pom at the front to make a beak. The beak should point down towards the feet as shown. Glue a wing on to each side of the chicken.

6 Trace the comb template on page 31 on to a sheet of white paper. Cut it out. Use the template to draw a comb on the red felt. Cut it out. Put a blob of glue on both sides of the straight edge and tuck it in between the folds on top of the chicken from front to back.

7 Glue on two googly eyes.

Snappy Croc

Better make it snappy! This crocodile hand puppet has two rows of sharp teeth – and it's coming your way!

For a snappy hand puppet you will need

- strip of green paper 68cm x 17cm
- double-sided sticky tape
- red paper 28cm x 12cm
- scissors
- 2 strips of white paper 17cm x 3cm
- bubble wrap 17cm x 17cm
- green paint
- paintbrush
- blue felt-tip pen
- glue
- 4 x polystyrene balls 2.5cm in diameter
- black paint and paintbrush
- pencil

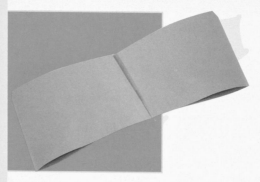

1 Fold the strip of green paper in half. Open it out. Fold each end into the middle. Crease along the fold line. Open it out. You will have four equal sections.

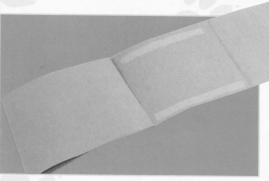

2 Cut a 15cm length of double-sided sticky tape. Stick it along the long, top edge of one of the two middle sections of your paper, 1cm away from the centre fold line. Repeat on the long, bottom edge of your paper. Fold the end section over on top of the sticky tape and press firmly down. Repeat on the other side of your long strip of paper. Turn the paper over. You will see that you have made two pockets. The pockets are the outside of the crocodile's head.

3 Fold the piece of red paper in half. Starting at the fold, draw half an oval. Cut out the oval shape.

4 Turn the green paper over again and glue the red oval in the middle of the green paper. Leave it to dry. Fold the paper in half with the red oval on the inside. This is the crocodiles's mouth.

inside

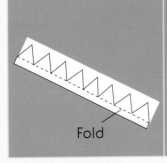

5 To make the teeth, draw a zig-zag on the strip of white paper as shown and a dotted line to show you where the paper will be folded. Cut out along the zig-zag line. Draw round the shape on to the other strip of white paper. Cut it out.

6 Fold the teeth just below the points. Glue the straight edge of one set of teeth along the outside of the folded edge of the paper as shown. Repeat at the opposite end of the paper.

7 Paint the bumpy side of the piece of bubble wrap green. Leave it to dry. Glue the unpainted side of the bubble wrap to the outside of the crocodile's head.

8 To make the eyes, paint a blue spot on two of the polystyrene balls. Glue the eyes on to the bubble wrap on each side at the back of the shape near the pocket opening.

Snap.........snap.......snap...........snap.....

9 Paint half of the other two polystyrene balls black. Leave them to dry. Paint the other half of the polystyrene balls green. Leave to dry. Glue them to the bubble wrap near to the teeth.

10 Slide your fingers in to the opening between the two pieces of paper, under the eyes. Put your thumb between the other two pieces of paper. Open and close the mouth with a snap!

Dancing Dragon

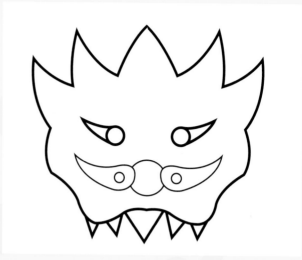

Chinese dragons are mythical creatures that bring good luck. In China the symbol of the dragon is seen everywhere, particularly at Chinese New Year. This dancing paper dragon is sure to give you good luck every day.

For your dancing dragon you will need

- sheet of thin white card
- felt-tip pens
- scissors
- long strips of coloured paper in different colours 5cm wide
- double-sided sticky tape
- 2 chopsticks or pencils
- sticky tape
- ribbons, crêpe paper strips or paper strips

1 Trace the template on page 31 on to thin white card. Cut it out around the outline.

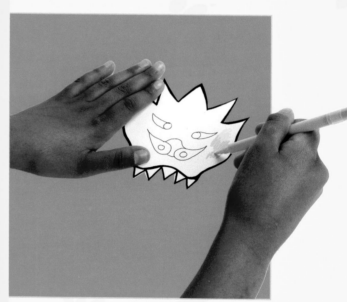

2 Colour in the shape using felt-tip pens.

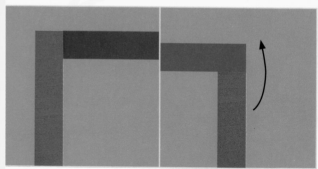

3 Take two strips of coloured paper and place them one on top of the other at right angles.

4 Fold the strip underneath up over the strip on top. Crease the fold.

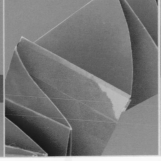
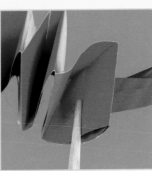

5 Fold the strip underneath up over the strip that is now on top.

6 Repeat until there is no spare strip left. You will have made a concertina shape. This is the body of your dragon.

7 To make a longer body attach two more strips using double-sided sticky tape. Continue to add strips until the body is as long as you want it to be.

8 Tape the chopsticks or pencils to the body, one at each end.

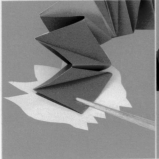
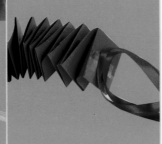

9 Use double-sided sticky tape to attach the head to the first square.

10 Tape thin ribbons, crêpe paper strips or strips of paper to the last square to make a tail.

Hold your dragon by the two sticks and make him dance.

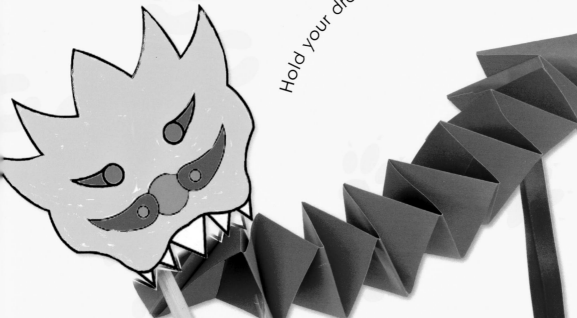

Cake-pop Piglets

Cake-pops are bite-size cakes on a stick. What better way to enjoy a sweet treat than with these cute piglet cake-pops?

For cake-pop piglets you will need

- half a chocolate sponge cake
- mixing bowl
- frosting (available in tubs from supermarkets)
- dessertspoon
- baking tray
- packet of strawberry cake-decorating buttons, melted as indicated in the instructions on the packet. Reserve a few for making the ears
- cake-pop sticks
- pink candy-coated chocolate buttons
- kitchen knife
- block of modelling clay
- tube of black writing icing

Ask a grown up to melt the strawberry cake-decorating buttons for you.

1 Break the cake up into fine crumbs in a mixing bowl.

2 Add two dessertspoons of frosting and mix with the cake crumbs until it all sticks together in a lump.

3 Break off a small piece of the mixture and roll it into a ball.

4 Put the ball of chocolate mixture on to a baking tray. Repeat step 3 until all the mixture is rolled into balls. Put the baking tray into the fridge for two hours to chill.

5 When the chocolate balls have chilled, prepare a quarter of the strawberry cake-decorating buttons. Dip the end of a stick into the melted chocolate.

6 Push the stick in to a ball of cake. Put it on to the baking tray. Repeat with all the rest of the chocolate balls. Put the baking tray back into the fridge until the sticks are set in the cake mixture.

7 When the sticks are set firm in the chocolate balls, prepare the rest of the strawberry buttons. Holding a stick, dip a cake-pop into the melted mixture. Turn it round until it is covered in chocolate. Tap the stick on the side of the bowl and let any excess mixture drip off. Push the sticks into the block of modelling clay and leave to set.

9 Cut one of the reserved strawberry buttons into quarters. Stick pieces into the mixture on either side of the top as ears. Stick a pink candy-coated button on to the front as a snout.

10 When the cake-pop has set, squeeze two dots of black icing on either side of the head for the eyes. Squeeze two dots of icing on to the pink candy-coated button for the nostrils.

Oink, oink, oink, oink!

Crazy Penguin Cards

Most penguins are black and white. This makes them hard to see when there are dark shadows on the snow. But this crazy penguin family has fantastic bright colours. These penguins will make lovely cards to send to your friends.

For a crazy penguin card you will need

- sheet of thin card (coloured or white)
- scissors
- thin coloured paper in green, pink, red, blue and purple
- sheet of thin yellow card 10cm x 20cm
- glue
- black felt-tip pen

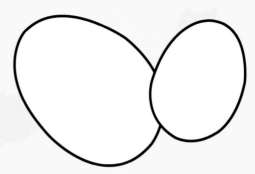

1 Using the templates on page 30 cut out from thin card one large and one smaller egg shape.

2 Draw round the smaller egg-shaped template on to thin green paper. Cut it out.

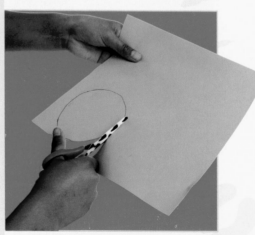

3 Repeat step 2 with the large egg-shaped template on thin pink paper.

4 Using the triangle templates, cut out two long red triangles, one small blue triangle and two small purple triangles.

5 Fold the yellow card in half to make a square. Glue the large pink egg shape on to the front.

6 Glue the smaller green egg shape on top of the pink one for the tummy.

7 Glue the long red triangles and the two purple triangles on the egg shape as shown.

8 Glue on a small blue triangle for the beak as shown.

9 Using the black felt-tip pen, draw two dots for eyes.

Some penguins have feathery plumes on their heads. You could add a spiky paper cut-out to these penguins.

You can use the templates again and again to make more penguin cards in lots of different colours.

Templates

Crazy Penguin Family
Pages 28 – 29

Pom-pom Animals
Pages 20 – 21

Big Cat Masks
Pages 4 – 5

Pom-pom
Animals
Pages 20 – 21

Dancing Dragon
Pages 24 – 35

Fish Kite
Pages 8 – 9

Furry Hamster
Pages 18 – 19

Back stitch

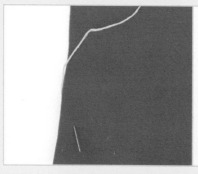 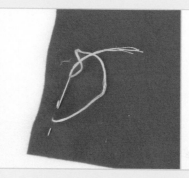 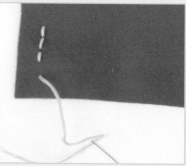

1 Thread the needle. Tie a knot in the end of the thread. Push the needle up from the back of the fabric. Pull the thread through to the knot.

2 Push the needle down through the fabric just behind where it came up. Push the needle up from the back to just in front of the first stitch and pull it through.

3 Push the needle back down to join up with the last stitch. A row of back stitches will all join up together.

Further Information

Books

Animals Instincts: series by Tom Jackson (Wayland, 2011)
Animals Are Amazing: series by Valerie Bodden (Franklin Watts, 2012)
Extreme Pets: series by Deborah Chancellor and Selina Wood (Franklin Watts, 2010)
Pets Plus: series by Sally Morgan and Honor Head (Franklin Watts, 2012

Websites

http://kids.nationalgeographic.com/kids/animals/creaturefeature/
http://gowild.wwf.org.uk/

Index